* cowhide

*duct tape

*kitty litter

* cray-cray!

* bulldozer

* reindeer

* plastic wrap

* feedback

* tycoon

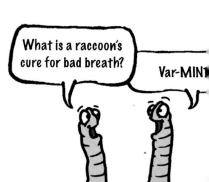

* mailbox

* egg drop soup

* nightfall

* spring break

* carpool

* abominable

* noble

* potty train

* ice cream

* curling iron

* styling mousse

* complementary colors

* white lies

* boredom

* stakeout

* catsup

* tie-dyed

* hairpiece

* bleu cheese

* dandelion

* believe

* goatee

* polygon

* cow tipping

* pig out

* the end